W9-DFG-662

DATE DUE

OCT 0 8 2011			
		MAY 2 3 2015	

Great Artists

Edgar Degas

ABDO
Publishing Company

Joanne Mattern

Edgar Degas

Edgar Degas was an artist who lived in Paris, France. He was part of a group of painters called the Impressionists. These artists created scenes of ordinary life. However, Degas's style was more traditional than the other Impressionists.

Degas's art was different for many reasons. For example, it was not impulsive. Instead, Degas drew from memory and arranged the figures to create just the right effect. And, he was able to capture the human figure in motion unlike any other artist.

Degas's favorite **medium** was pastel, but he did more than just paint. He also took photographs and made **prints**. Later in life, he also made wax sculptures.

People were amazed at how many different things this artist created. Degas had hidden many works in his studio that were not found until after his death. His art is still enjoyed by people around the world.

Edgar Degas was never satisfied with his art. He was always reworking his paintings.

Timeline

1834 ~ Hilaire-Germain-Edgar Degas was born on July 19.

1845 ~ Degas entered the Lycée Louis-le-Grand.

1853 ~ Degas graduated from the lycée.

1855 ~ Degas entered the École des Beaux-Arts in Paris.

1860 ~ Degas finished *The Bellelli Family*.

1867 ~ Degas exhibited at the Paris Salon for the first time.

1869 ~ Degas painted *At the Races in the Countryside*.

1870s ~ Degas began painting ballet scenes.

1873 ~ Degas finished painting the *New Orleans Cotton Office*.

1874 ~ The Impressionists had their first art show.

1917 ~ On September 27, Degas died in Paris.

Fun Facts

- Edgar Degas was one of the leading art collectors of his time.

- Édouard Manet once slashed a painting that Degas had made of Manet and his wife. Manet did not think his wife had been portrayed in a flattering manner. So, he cut her face from the canvas. When Degas saw his ruined painting, he took the canvas down and left without a word.

- In 1832, Degas's father, Auguste, changed the family name to De Gas to give the appearance of status. Degas went back to the original spelling in the 1860s.

- Degas admired Jean-Auguste-Dominique Ingres. Ingres was a French painter who was known for his portraits and historical paintings. Degas was lucky enough to meet Ingres. When Degas told Ingres that he was a painter, Ingres said, "Draw lines . . . lots of lines, either from memory or from nature."

Young Edgar

Edgar Degas was born in Paris on July 19, 1834. His full name was Hilaire-Germain-Edgar, but everyone called him Edgar. He was the oldest child in the Degas family. Edgar had two brothers, Achille and René. He also had two sisters named Thérèse and Marguerite.

Edgar's parents were Auguste and Célestine. The Degas family was very rich. Edgar's grandfather had founded a bank in Naples, Italy. Auguste ran the Paris office of this large bank.

When Edgar was 11 years old, his parents sent him to one of the best-known secondary schools in Paris. It was called the Lycée Louis-le-Grand.

While at the lycée, Edgar studied many different things. His classes included French literature, Latin, Greek, music, and drawing. Edgar liked school and studied with enthusiasm.

Edgar loved Paris and its people.
He painted many pictures of people
who lived and worked there.

A Love of Art

When Edgar was 13 years old, his mother died. However, Edgar and his father got along very well. Edgar referred to Auguste as "dear papa." On Sunday mornings, Auguste often met Edgar at school. The two would spend the day visiting Paris's art museums and art collectors.

Paris has many museums filled with different kinds of art. The most well-known museum is the Louvre. Edgar and Auguste often visited this museum.

Edgar also went to the Louvre by himself. He liked to copy the famous paintings he found there. Some of his favorites were by **Renaissance** artists.

Auguste also had many friends who were artists, musicians, and art collectors. Sometimes, he took Edgar with him when he visited these friends. Edgar enjoyed looking at the art in their homes.

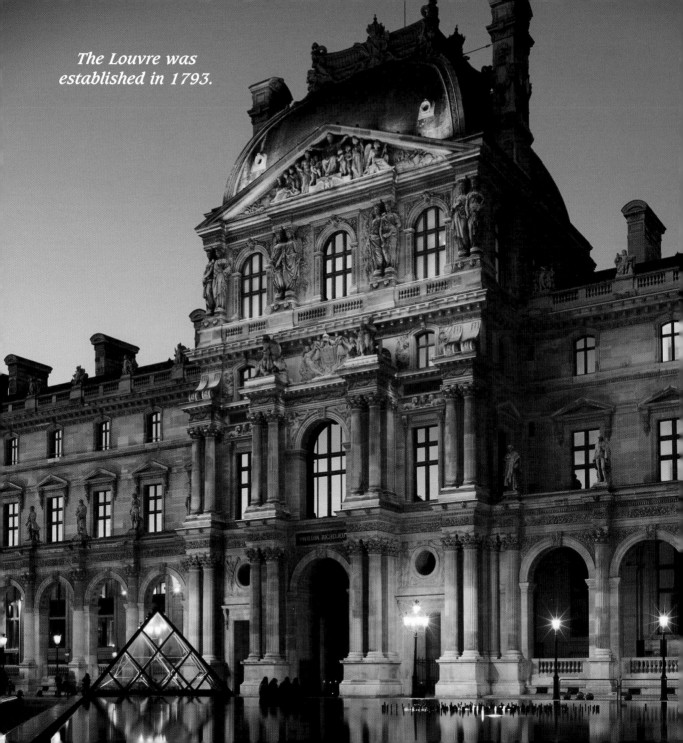

The Louvre was established in 1793.

A Big Decision

Edgar was 19 when he graduated from the Lycée Louis-le-Grand. Now he could study at a university. Auguste wanted Edgar to become a lawyer. He hoped that Edgar would take over the bank someday.

Edgar had other ideas. He wanted to become an artist. However, his father was not happy about this choice. So to please Auguste, Edgar entered law school.

Instead of going to class, Edgar often went to the Louvre to copy paintings. He soon dropped out of law school. He told his father that he had to become a painter. Finally, Auguste agreed that Edgar could go to art school.

In 1855, Edgar entered the École des Beaux-Arts in Paris. This was one of the oldest and best art schools in the world. Edgar began to study with a teacher named Louis Lamothe.

Edgar was inspired by the clean lines in Jean-Auguste-Dominique Ingres's paintings.

Lamothe had been a student of Edgar's **idol**, Jean-Auguste-Dominique Ingres. Lamothe inspired Edgar's love of drawing. And, he encouraged Edgar to continue studying the **Renaissance** artists.

Growing Artist

Degas enjoyed studying with Lamothe. He also spent a lot of time at the Louvre. He tried to make his artwork look just like the paintings hanging on the walls. Degas felt this was an excellent way to learn how to become an artist.

Historians are unsure how long Degas attended the École des Beaux-Arts. However it is known that in 1856, Degas traveled to Italy to study art. He spent almost three years there. While he was in Italy, Degas copied the artwork he found in Italy's art museums and churches.

Degas also had relatives in Italy, and he enjoyed spending time with them. He painted several portraits of his relatives. Then, Degas decided to create a family portrait. Degas spent months on the portrait's sketches.

Young Edgar Degas

While in Italy, Degas visited Rome. Its buildings have inspired artists for centuries.

Degas sent some of the art he worked on in Italy back to his father in France. Auguste was very pleased with Degas's work. He said that Degas had a great future as an artist.

Degas was not so sure. He wondered if he would ever become a great artist. He frequently worried and spent a lot of time by himself.

Change in Style

Degas returned to Paris in 1859. That fall, he rented a studio where he could paint. Then, Degas began combining the sketches of his Italian relatives into one painting.

Degas finished his family portrait in 1860. It was called *The Bellelli Family*. The portrait shows a sad, tense family. Degas exhibited the painting at the Paris Salon in 1867. He then put it away in his studio.

Degas continued to visit the Louvre for inspiration. During a visit there in the early 1860s, he had met a painter named Édouard Manet.

Of his friends, Édouard Manet and Mary Cassatt were Degas's favorite subjects. Degas took a particular interest in this drawing of Manet.

The two artists had much in common and had become friends.

One thing Degas and Manet had in common was what they wanted to paint. They wanted to show life as it happened. Both men knew other artists who were also tired of painting traditional scenes in greens, browns, and grays.

Degas and his friends began a new art movement that became known as Impressionism. Like the other Impressionists, Degas's paintings became more colorful and lively. But unlike the others, Degas created his scenes from notes.

Manet inspired many of the Impressionists with his art. He never exhibited with them. However, he did employ many of their painting techniques, including painting at the scene.

At the Racetrack

There were many common themes shown by Impressionists. One of these themes was horse racing. In the 1860s, this sport was becoming a popular social event in France. Degas liked to attend races and often made many sketches of the horses and **jockeys**.

Degas liked to show the animals before they raced. He often painted the crowds, too. His 1869 painting *At the Races in the Countryside* creates a realistic image of a moment in time. It shows a family in a horse-drawn carriage with jockeys and their horses in a green field behind it.

At the Races in the Countryside *was inspired by one of Degas's visits to the races.*

A study of a galloping horse

Degas admired the quick and graceful movements of the horses. He realized that in order to make his subjects come alive he needed to see **three-dimensional** images. So, he began sculpting them in order to learn more about their movements.

Degas's interest in modern life and his love of motion is seen in his racetrack scenes. Then in the 1870s, Degas began to paint with the eye of a cameraman. To do this, he created unusual figure groupings. And, parts of some of the figures were cut off by the frame.

At the Ballet

Along with horse races, Degas also enjoyed going to the ballet. He attended performances and sat in on **rehearsals**. Beginning in the early 1870s, Degas began painting ballet scenes. He painted the ballerinas practicing, resting, and lacing their shoes.

Degas tried to capture every aspect of a dancer's life. His paintings showed natural moments taken from real life. However, he painted very few pictures of dancers onstage during a show.

Degas wanted his ballet paintings to be **accurate**. So, he learned different ballet steps and positions in order to paint them better. Degas had a notebook filled with different ballet positions.

Degas's ballet paintings were an immediate success. In time, Degas became known as "the painter of dancers." He created about 1,500 paintings, pastels, drawings, and sculptures with the dance theme.

Artist's Corner

The differences between Degas and other Impressionists can be seen in his ballet scenes. He did not draw what he saw as it had happened, like other Impressionists. Instead, Degas drew indoor, carefully planned scenes. To do this, he made many different sketches and then created one painting out of them.

Degas also liked to portray the unexpected. He painted his dancers in positions that make the viewer believe the ballerinas did not know they were models. He did not make the girls into glamorous figures. In fact, he was often criticized for displaying common-looking subjects. He showed the girls tired and fixing their clothes more often than onstage during a performance.

In his paintings, Degas experimented with technique and size. Some works show many figures in a small space. Others have wide-open floors, with just a few figures in the background, such as *Waiting: Dancer and Woman with Umbrella on a Bench* (right). And, he shows the dancers from unusual angles in order to emphasize certain elements, as in *Dancer Fastening Her Pump* (left).

Trip to America

In 1870, France went to war with Prussia, which is now part of Germany. Degas joined the National Guard and served during the war. Paris suffered terribly during this war, and many people were killed.

After a peace treaty was signed in 1871, Paris still faced difficult times. Degas decided to leave the city for a while. He and his brother René traveled to the United States. They visited some relatives in New Orleans, Louisiana.

Degas enjoyed seeing his family. He painted many pictures of them. "What a good thing family is," he wrote in a letter. However, Degas was soon bored and homesick.

Degas's American relatives worked in the cotton business. And, he grew tired of all the talk about cotton. He missed the ballet, the theater, and the familiarity of Paris, too.

Early in 1873, Degas returned to Paris. He lived there for the rest of his life. However, his experience in Louisiana led him to paint the *New Orleans Cotton Office* in 1873.

New Orleans Cotton Office *is Degas's best-known movement scene.*

Shocking News

In 1874, Degas's father died. Degas discovered that Auguste had not done a very good job of running the bank. The family had to pay back the money the bank had lost.

Degas took responsibility for paying the family's **debts**. Until then, he had not needed to work for a living. For the first time, Degas would have to sell his paintings to earn money.

At this time, the Impressionists were organizing their own exhibition. Most French artists displayed their work at the Paris Salon. However, the Impressionists did not want to follow the strict style rules of the Salon judges. Instead, they decided to have their own show.

Degas agreed to show his work with the Impressionists. This allowed him to display many of his paintings at one time. He included ten works in the show.

The Impressionists' exhibition was not a success. Few people came, and there were few sales. Those who attended laughed and made fun of the artwork. Despite the attacks by **critics**, Degas received a good amount of praise for his works.

Competition

Impressionists often painted similar themes. Manet and Degas competed to see who could capture each theme the best. In Manet's Music Lesson, his figures are stiff with no interaction between the man and the woman. Manet focused on the contrast between light and dark. His painting follows the more traditional patterns. These patterns include concentration on light, form, and color.

On the other hand, Degas followed the Impressionistic style by portraying reality. Violinist and Young Woman shows a room filled with sunlight. And, he focused on the posture of the two figures in relation to each other. The woman in Degas's painting looks like she is caught in the middle of something. This painting shows his love of motion.

Manet's Music Lesson (top) **and Degas's** Violinist and Young Woman (bottom)

Art Experiments

Throughout his career, Degas experimented with different **mediums** and **techniques**. He would try anything to create just the right painting.

At first, Degas used oil paints to create his work. Later, he used colored crayons called pastels. Then, he mixed pastels with **charcoal** and different kinds of paint. Sometimes, Degas even blew steam from a kettle onto his pastels to create various effects.

Degas also enjoyed taking pictures. He liked to explore the effects of light on images. Many people thought his paintings looked like photos. Sometimes, parts of objects were cut off in his paintings, just as they might be in a photograph.

Degas's experiments with painting techniques created rich paintings.

In 1877, Degas met an artist named Mary Cassatt. Cassatt admired Degas. She once said, "The first sight of Degas's pictures, was the turning point in my artistic life." Degas taught Cassatt the art of making **prints**. He also relied on her to find clients to buy his art.

Later in her life, Cassatt expressed dislike for this portrait Degas had made of her. She did not want to leave it to her family as a representation of herself. She was offended by the unladylike pose.

Later Years

Degas never married or had children. He was close to several artists. However, many people said that Degas was a grumpy man. He was known for his stubborn views on art and his harsh remarks.

As Degas got older, he began to lose his eyesight. He could not see well enough to paint as much as he used to. Instead, he made sculptures out of wax.

One of these sculptures is called *The Little 14-Year-Old Dancer*. It is a ballerina that he dressed in real clothing and ballet slippers. He even gave it real hair tied with a satin ribbon. This was the only sculpture Degas showed in public.

Degas's sculptures were restored and cast in bronze after his death.

Edgar Degas died on September 27, 1917. He was 83 years old and almost blind. After Degas died, people were surprised to find many more wax sculptures inside his studio. The studio was also packed with hundreds of works of art.

Degas had been able to live his dream of painting the world around him and showing it to others. His art was popular and admired. His work helped people see ordinary things in a new way.

Today, Degas is known for his works done in the ballet and racetrack themes.

Glossary

accurate - free of errors. Something with errors is inaccurate.

charcoal - a black, soft material that is a form of carbon.

critic - a professional who gives his or her opinion on art or performances.

debt - something owed to someone, usually money.

idol - a figure that others look up to and respect.

jockey - a person who rides a horse in a race.

medium - a mode of artistic expression.

print - a reproduction of an original work of art.

rehearsal - a private performance in preparation for a public appearance.

Renaissance - a revival of art and learning that began in Italy during the fourteenth century, marked by a renewed interest in Greek and Latin literature and art.

technique - a method or style in which something is done.

three-dimensional - having the illusion of depth.

Saying It

Cassatt - kuh-SAT
École des Beaux-Arts - AYKOLE day BOHZAHR
Édouard Manet - AY-DWAWR MAW-NEH
Hilaire-Germain-Edgar Degas - EE-LEHR-ZHEHR-MAN-ED-GAWR DUH-GAH
Jean-Auguste-Dominique Ingres - ZHAHN-AW-GOOST-DAW-MEE-NEEK ANGRUH
Louis Lamothe - LWEE lah-MOHT
Louvre - LOOV
lycée - lee-SAY
Renaissance - reh-nuh-SAHNS

Web Sites

To learn more about Edgar Degas, visit ABDO Publishing Company on the World Wide Web at **www.abdopub.com**. Web sites about Degas are featured on our Book Links page. These links are routinely monitored and updated to provide the most current information available.

Index